THE**BLAZING**CENTER

STUDY GUIDE

DESIRING GOD

Multnomah Books

THE BLAZING CENTER STUDY GUIDE
published by Multnomah Books
A division of Random House, Inc.

© 2006 by Desiring God Ministries

International Standard Book Number: 1-59052-685-6

Cover design by Studiogearbox.com

Unless otherwise indicated, Scripture quotations are from:
The Holy Bible, *English Standard Version* (ESV)
© 2001 by Crossway Bibles, a division of Good News Publishers.
Used by permission. All rights reserved.

Multnomah is a trademark of Multnomah Publishers
and is registered in the U.S. Patent and Trademark Office.
The colophon is a trademark of Multnomah Publishers.

Printed in the United States of America

For information:
MULTNOMAH BOOKS
12265 ORACLE BOULEVARD, SUITE 200
COLORADO SPRINGS, CO 80921

07 08 09 10—10 9 8 7 6 5

CONTENTS

INTRODUCTION TO THIS STUDY GUIDE

Avery real and very serious battle is being waged for our eternal destiny. The assault that we face every day is not in the form of bullets, grenades, or poisonous gas. No, the weapons brought against us are more subtle and far more deadly. The evil one attacks us through television and computer screens, in the books we read, in the whispers of our peers, through mirrors, music, and magazines. The lies of the flesh are everywhere and sin's allurements cannot be totally avoided.

But in the swirl of glitz and flash and skin and swagger and muscle,[1] 1 Thessalonians 5:23–24 stands unmoved as a beacon of hope: "Now may the God of peace himself sanctify you completely, and may your whole spirit and soul and body be kept blameless at the coming of our Lord Jesus Christ. He who calls you is faithful; he will surely do it." God is faithful to his children. He can protect their faith and he can grant them a radical, counter-cultural witness in this generation.

It is our prayer that God would be pleased to use this study guide to raise up an army of God-centered, Christ-exalting men and women who know a joy that this world cannot match and cannot touch. It is our desire that countless lives would, by the undeserved and all powerful grace of God, be changed forever.

This study guide is designed to be used in a ten-session, guided group study that focuses on *The Blazing Center* DVD set.[2] After an introductory lesson, each subsequent lesson examines one 30-minute session from *The Blazing Center*. You, the learner, are encouraged to use the week prior to prepare for the viewing of each session by reading and reflecting upon Scripture, by considering key quotations, and by asking yourself penetrating questions. Your preparatory work for each lesson is marked with the heading "Before You Watch the DVD, Study and Prepare" in Lessons 2–9.

The workload is conveniently divided into five daily (and, we hope, manageable) assignments. There is also a section suggesting further study. This work is to be completed individually before the group convenes to view the DVD and discuss the material.

> Throughout this study guide, paragraphs printed in a shaded box (like this one) are excerpts from a book written by John Piper, or excerpts taken from the Desiring God website (www.desiringGod.org). They are included to supplement the study questions and to summarize key or provocative points.

The next section in Lessons 2–9, entitled "While You Watch the DVD, Take Notes," is to be completed as the DVD is playing. You are encouraged to engage with the DVD by filling in the appropriate blanks and writing down other notes that will aid you in the group discussion. The third section in these weekly lessons is "After You Watch the DVD, Discuss What You've Learned." Three discussion questions are provided to guide and focus the conversation. You may record, in the spaces provided here, notes that will help you contribute to the conversation. Or, you may use this space to record things from the discussion that you want to remember.

The final section is an application section: "After You Discuss, Make Application." You will be challenged to record a "take-away point" and to engage in a certain activity that is a fitting response to the content presented in the lesson.

Group leaders should also read through the Leader's Guide, included at the end of this study guide.

As we've said, life transformation will only occur by the grace of God. Therefore, we highly encourage you to pray throughout the learning process. Pray that God would open your mind to see wonderful things in his Word. Pray that he would grant you the insight, concentration, and attention you need in order to benefit from this resource. Pray that God would cause you to rejoice in the truth. And pray that the discussion in your group would be mutually encouraging and edifying. We've included specific objectives at the beginning of each lesson. These objectives won't be realized without the gracious work of God through prayer.

May the soul-satisfying supremacy of God in all things be seen and savored through this resource!

INTRODUCTION TO
THE BLAZING CENTER

LESSON OBJECTIVES

It is our prayer that after you have finished this lesson...

- You will get a feel for how you and others in your group approach the glory of God and personal joy.

- Your curiosity would be roused, and questions would begin to come to mind.

- You will be eager to learn more about your joy and God's glory.

ABOUT YOURSELF

1. What is your name?
2. Tell the group something about yourself that they probably don't already know.
3. Describe your relationship with Jesus.

A PREVIEW OF *THE BLAZING CENTER*

LESSON 1

1. What is the place of the emotions in Christianity? Are proper emotions essential to being a Christian or are they optional? Explain. What emotions are proper for Christians?

2. Do you want to be happy? Is that a bad thing? Why or why not? Should your desire to be happy motivate everything you do, or does God sometimes call you to suppress your desire to be happy in order to do the "right thing"?

THE BLAZING CENTER: A PERSONAL STORY

A Companion Study to *The Blazing Center*, Session 1

LESSON OBJECTIVES

It is our prayer that after you have finished this lesson...

- A passion for the glory of God will be awakened in your soul.

- You will begin to think about how your joy relates to the glory of God.

- You will understand more fully why God sent his Son, Jesus, to the cross.

Before You Watch the DVD, Study and Prepare

DAY 1—YOUR PERSONAL STORY

LESSON 2

DAY 1

In Session 1 of *The Blazing Center*, John Piper tells us a little bit about his teenage years. He shares about his desire to be happy and about his reverence for the glory of God.

John Piper recalls much unrest and heartache during these years. But God's grace was at work in his life:

> I think the grace of God took every day's pain, and used it for my good—and yours. What a difference, if I had not spent certain fall afternoons staring out across Dellwood valley toward Piney Mountain listening to the distant trains and wondering what it would be like to get on one and go where nobody would wonder why the preacher's kid can't even give a book report. What a difference, if I had never sat alone under the dogwood tree and tried to write a poem for my mother to somehow help her feel that I felt she was the only one in all the world who seemed to understand. What a difference if my teenage years had been smooth! But instead God clogged my mouth in order to fill my heart.
>
> So I testify to all of you today: I have seen the grace of God in my life and I am glad. He takes what seems to be the worst of circumstances and turns them into good news.[3]

Question 1: Do you desire to be happy? How do you know? How does your happiness figure into all the decisions that you make every day? Record your reflections.

Question 2: What does the phrase, "the glory of God," bring to your mind first? What does the glory of God have to do with you?

DAY 2—WHAT GOD IS PASSIONATE ABOUT

Very few people ask what *God* is passionate about. But isn't this one of the most important questions that you can ask?

[W]e tend to be more familiar with our duties than with God's designs. We know why we exist—to glorify God and enjoy him forever. But why does God exist? What should he love with all his heart and soul and mind and strength?[4]

LESSON
2

DAY
2

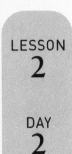

LESSON
2

DAY
2

Question 3: What do you think God is passionate about? What do you think God is *most* passionate about? Can you think of any Bible verses to back up your answer?

Question 4: Study Isaiah 48:8–11.

8 You have never heard, you have never known, from of old your ear has not been opened. For I knew that you would surely deal treacherously, and that from before birth you were called a rebel. 9 For my name's sake I defer my anger, for the sake of my praise I restrain it for you, that I may not cut you off. 10 Behold, I have refined you, but not as silver; I have tried you in the furnace of affliction. 11 For my own sake, for my own sake, I do it, for how should my name be profaned? My glory I will not give to another.

According to these verses, what is God passionate about? Record your answer and specific verses to support your answer.

DAY 3—WHY IS THE UNIVERSE SO BIG?

How many stars can you see from your house on a clear night? Have you ever looked into the night sky and wondered why the universe is so big?

Question 5: If you had to guess…

- How many miles across is the Milky Way galaxy?

  _____

- How many stars are in our galaxy?

  _____

- How many known galaxies are there in the universe?

  _____

Question 6: Look at Psalm 19:1.

> 1 The heavens declare the glory of God, and the sky above proclaims his handiwork.

According to this verse, why does the universe exist?

LESSON
2

DAY
3

Now look at Job 26:7–14.

**LESSON
2**

**DAY
3**

7 He stretches out the north over the void and hangs the earth on nothing. 8 He binds up the waters in his thick clouds, and the cloud is not split open under them. 9 He covers the face of the full moon and spreads over it his cloud. 10 He has inscribed a circle on the face of the waters at the boundary between light and darkness. 11 The pillars of heaven tremble and are astounded at his rebuke. 12 By his power he stilled the sea; by his understanding he shattered Rahab. 13 By his wind the heavens were made fair; his hand pierced the fleeing serpent. 14 Behold, these are but the outskirts of his ways, and how small a whisper do we hear of him! But the thunder of his power who can understand?

Why might the universe be so big?

DAY 4—FALLING SHORT

Question 7: Romans 3:23 declares that "all have sinned and fall short of the glory of God." What is the relationship between sinning and falling short of the glory of God?

Question 8: Which of the following is the best biblical definition of sin?

a. messing up or making a mistake
b. hurting someone else
c. failing to live for the glory of God
d. doing what the law says not to do

What does it mean to "fall short" of the glory of God? It does not mean that we are supposed to be as glorious as God is and have fallen short. We ought to fall short in that sense! The best explanation of Romans 3:23 is Romans 1:23. It says that those who did not glorify or thank God became fools "and exchanged the glory of the immortal God for images." This is the way we "fall short" of the glory of God: We exchange it for something of lesser value. All sin comes from not putting supreme value on the glory of God—this is the very essence of sin.[5]

LESSON
2

DAY
4

DAY 5—SHOULD GOD BE KICKED OFF THE BENCH?

Psalm 7:11 says that "God is a righteous judge." But can a righteous judge let criminals go free?

Question 9: Imagine that you are in a courtroom near where you live and a convicted murderer is standing before the judge. There is no doubt in anyone's mind that this murderer deserves to be severely punished. But the judge looks directly at the murderer and says, "You can go free. I forgive you." How would you react?

Question 10: If Jesus hadn't died, then would God be able to forgive sins? Why not? Read Romans 3:21–26, especially concentrating on verse 25.

21 But now the righteousness of God has been manifested apart from the law, although the Law and the Prophets bear witness to it— 22 the righteousness of God through faith in Jesus Christ for all who believe. For there is no distinction: 23 for all have sinned and fall short of the glory of God, 24 and are justified by his grace as a gift, through the redemption that is in Christ Jesus, 25 whom God put forward as a propitiation by his blood, to be received by faith. This was to show God's righteousness, because in his divine forbearance he

had passed over former sins. [26] It was to show his righteousness at the present time, so that he might be just and the justifier of the one who has faith in Jesus.

According to these verses, why was it necessary for Jesus to die for sins?

FURTHER UP AND FURTHER IN

Note: The "Further Up and Further In" section is for those who want to study more. It is a section for further reference and going deeper. The phrase "further up and further in" is borrowed from C. S. Lewis.

Read *Desiring God*, Chapter 1, pages 31–44

The beginning of this chapter defends the idea that "God is uppermost in His own affections" (page 31) and that the foundation for his happiness is his total sovereignty.

Question 11: According to this section, why is God's happiness necessary for our happiness?

Question 12: If God is completely sovereign, does that mean he is responsible for the evil in the world?

LESSON

2

Further up and further in

Study John Piper's Mission Statement

"I exist to spread a passion for the supremacy of God in all things for the joy of all peoples through Jesus Christ."

Question 13: Why do you suppose the word "passion" is chosen? Why couldn't the mission statement read, "I exist to spread an *understanding* of the supremacy of God…"?

Question 14: Why is the "joy of all peoples" so important? Should their joy be our mission?

Read *Desiring God*, Appendix 1, "The Goal of God in Redemptive History"

Question 15: List all the texts in this appendix which demonstrate that God does all things for the sake of his glory.

While You Watch the DVD, Take Notes

John Piper's mission statement:

> To spread a _____ for the _____ of God in
> all things for the_____ of all peoples through Jesus Christ.

What two things was God creating in John Piper during his teenage years?

1. _____
2. _____ really loves God's glory

According to John Piper, what is the universe about?

According to John Piper, what was the cross about?

After You Watch the DVD, Discuss What You've Learned

1. Interact with this statement: "As a Christian, you ought to seek as much happiness as you can possibly have."

2. What is one thing that stuck out to you about John Piper's description of his teenage years? Why did this grab your attention?

LESSON
2

DVD and discussion

LESSON

2

DVD
and
discussion

3. Do you agree that God created the universe and sent his Son to die *in order to glorify himself?* Defend your answer with Bible verses.

After You Discuss, Make Application

1. Record one thing from this lesson that you want to remember or think more about:

2. Compose a prayer asking God to give you a soft and teachable heart. Ask that he would guide you as you study his Word and work through this resource. Plead with God that he would be glorified in your life and affections. Record your prayer here:

THE BLAZING CENTER: IS GOD VAIN?

A Companion Study to *The Blazing Center*, Session 2

LESSON OBJECTIVES

It is our prayer that after you have finished this lesson…

- You will be able to explain the way in which we "magnify" God.

- You will be able to define love biblically.

- You will understand how God can love us by glorifying himself.

Before You Watch the DVD, Study and Prepare

DAY 1—WHY IS JESUS COMING BACK?

LESSON
3

DAY
1

In the previous session of *The Blazing Center*, John Piper argued that God's intention at the beginning of history (the creation) and at the middle of history (the cross) was to glorify himself. Everything God does, he does to glorify himself.

> My conclusion is that God's own glory is uppermost in His own affections. In everything He does, His purpose is to preserve and display that glory. To say that His own glory is uppermost in His own affections means that He puts a greater value on it than on anything else. He delights in His glory above all things.[6]

Question 1: Why do you think that Jesus is coming back? What will God's purpose be at the end of history, when Jesus returns?

Question 2: Study 1 Thessalonians 1:9–10 and 4:16–17.

[9] For they themselves report concerning us the kind of reception we had among you, and how you turned to God from idols to serve the living and true God, [10] and to wait for his Son from heaven, whom he raised from the dead, Jesus who delivers us from the wrath to come.

Now look at 1 Thessalonians 4:16–17

16 For the Lord himself will descend from heaven with a cry of command, with the voice of an archangel, and with the sound of the trumpet of God. And the dead in Christ will rise first. 17 Then we who are alive, who are left, will be caught up together with them in the clouds to meet the Lord in the air, and so we will always be with the Lord.

According to these verses, why is Jesus coming back?

DAY 2—WHAT IS LOVE?

From the radio to the television, from poetry to advertisements, from pop psychology to teenage crushes, the language of love is everywhere, and it seems as if everyone has their own opinion about what it is. In the midst of pop-culture, however, the biblical portrayal of God's love may be surprising.

Question 3: How would you define or describe love? Record your reflections:

LESSON
3

DAY
2

Question 4: What do you think is the prevalent definition of love in our culture? How is your definition different from the world's definition?

> I ask people wherever I go: Do you feel loved by God because you believe he makes much of you, or because you believe he frees you and empowers you to enjoy making much of him?[7]

DAY 3—THE THING THAT WILL SATISFY YOUR SOUL

Question 5: What do you daydream about? In other words, when you imagine the best possible future, what happens? Who are you and what do you do?

One of the saddest feelings in the world is the feeling that your life is going nowhere. You're alive. But you feel like there is no point in being alive. You get a little daydream—a little flicker—of what it might be like to be a part of something really great and really valuable, and what it might be like to have a significant part in it. But then you wake up and everything looks so small and insignificant and pitiful and out of the way and unknown and pointless.

We were not made to live without a destiny. We were made to be sustained by a meaningful, purposeful future. We were made to be strengthened each day by this assurance, this confidence: that what is happening in our lives today, no matter how mundane and ordinary, is a really significant step toward something great and good and beautiful tomorrow.[8]

Question 6: What does your answer to the previous question say about what you think will bring you happiness? What will satisfy your soul most deeply and for the longest period of time?

LESSON
3

DAY
3

LESSON

3

DAY

4

Question 7: Based on your two previous answers, how would you define love? Can a person withhold what is truly good for someone else and still love them?

DAY 4—DOES GOD HAVE AN EGO?

Question 8: Imagine that you are at a party. One of your friends begins to list all of the great things he has done and how special he is. He then invites others to pay him compliments. Not only that, but he commands you to praise him and threatens to hurt you if you refuse. How would you react to such a person?

Question 9: Read Jeremiah 13:6–11.

6 And after many days the LORD said to me, "Arise, go to the Euphrates, and take from there the loincloth that I commanded you to hide there." 7 Then I went to the Euphrates, and dug, and I took the loincloth from the place where I had hidden it. And behold, the loincloth was spoiled; it was good for nothing. 8 Then the word of the LORD came to me: 9 "Thus says the LORD: Even so will I spoil the pride of Judah and the

great pride of Jerusalem. 10 This evil people, who refuse to hear my words, who stubbornly follow their own heart and have gone after other gods to serve them and worship them, shall be like this loincloth, which is good for nothing. 11 For as the loincloth clings to the waist of a man, so I made the whole house of Israel and the whole house of Judah cling to me, declares the LORD, that they might be for me a people, a name, a praise, and a glory, but they would not listen."

How is God similar to or different from the person described in the previous question?

DAY 5—PUZZLING VERSES FROM JOHN

Question 10: Reflect on John 11:1–7.

1 Now a certain man was ill, Lazarus of Bethany, the village of Mary and her sister Martha. 2 It was Mary who anointed the Lord with ointment and wiped his feet with her hair, whose brother Lazarus was ill. 3 So the sisters sent to him, saying, "Lord, he whom you love is ill." 4 But when Jesus heard it he said, "This illness does not lead to death. It is for the glory of God, so that the Son of God may be glorified through it." 5 Now Jesus loved Martha and her sister and Lazarus. 6 So, when he heard that Lazarus was ill, he stayed two days longer in the place where he was. 7 Then after this he said to the disciples, "Let us go to Judea again."

LESSON
3

DAY
5

*Further up
and
further in*

How does verse 5 relate to verse 6? If Jesus really loved Mary, Martha, and Lazarus, why did he stay "two days longer in the place where he was"?

FURTHER UP AND FURTHER IN

Study 2 Thessalonians 1:9–10

9 They will suffer the punishment of eternal destruction, away from the presence of the Lord and from the glory of his might, 10 when he comes on that day to be glorified in his saints, and to be marveled at among all who have believed, because our testimony to you was believed.

Question 11: According to these verses, why is Jesus coming back?

Question 12: How do these three statements relate (logically)?

a. Jesus is coming back to deliver us from the wrath to come.
b. Jesus is coming back so that we will always be with the Lord.
c. Jesus is coming back to be glorified and marveled at.

Read *Desiring God*, Chapter 1, pages 44–50

Question 13: According to this section, how can God be totally committed to glorifying himself and at the same time be absolutely loving toward us?

Read an Open Letter John Piper Wrote to a Man Named Michael Prowse
It can be found at:
http://www.desiringgod.org/ResourceLibrary/TasteAndSee/ByDate/2003/1245_An_Open_Letter_to_Michael_Prowse/

Question 14: Summarize Michael Prowse's problem with (the biblical) God in your own words.

Question 15: If you had to choose one sentence in this letter that summarized John Piper's response, which sentence would you choose? Why?

LESSON
3

Further up and further in

While You Watch the DVD, Take Notes

LESSON
3

*DVD
and
discussion*

Jesus is coming to be _____ and to be _____
_____.

How does a microscope magnify something?

How does a telescope magnify something?

When we "magnify" God, do we magnify like a microscope or like a telescope?

What will satisfy your soul most deeply and for the longest period of time?

Would God be loving if he withheld this from you?

John Piper thinks that the world's definition of love is: _____

John Piper's own definition of love is:_____

Love is _____ making much of someone; love is doing whatever you have to do in order to enthrall someone with what will make them _____ _____.

After You Watch the DVD, Discuss What You've Learned

1. What have been the most joyous moments of your life thus far? Were you thinking about yourself at these moments? Does this confirm John Piper's statement, "We were not made for mirrors"?

2. Explain the significance of this statement: "God is most glorified in you when you are most satisfied in him."

3. Is this a loving prayer: "Father, I desire that they also, whom you have given me, may be with me where I am, to see my glory that you have given me because you loved me before the foundation of the world" (John 17:24)? Defend your answer.

After You Discuss, Make Application

1. Record one thing from this lesson that you want to remember or think more about:

2. Share this statement with a Christian friend or family member: "God is most glorified in you when you are most satisfied in him." Explain to them what it means, and record your conversation here:

LESSON
3

DVD
and
discussion

PURSUE YOUR JOY: ISN'T THAT HEDONISM?

A Companion Study to *The Blazing Center*, Session 3

LESSON OBJECTIVES

I t is our prayer that after you have finished this lesson…

- You will grasp why pursuing God's glory and your own joy are not at odds.

- You will understand how to glorify God in your dying.

- You will be able to define Christian Hedonism.

Before You Watch the DVD, Study and Prepare

DAY 1—*THE BLAZING CENTER*

In this session, John Piper argues that it is crucial to fix God's glory as *The Blazing Center* of your solar system. Until God's glory is central in your mind and affections, all the planets in your life will be out of orbit. Therefore, our first task is to be radically God-centered.

> The solar system of our soul and our society was made to orbit around the glory of God as its all-controlling sun. And the entire human race has exchanged the glory of God for weightless, substitute satellites that have no gravity and can hold nothing in its proper orbit. Therefore all the world is disordered and decaying and moving toward destruction.[9]

Question 1: What is wrong, if anything, with this statement about Jesus' crucifixion: "Oh how valuable I must have been that he died for me"?

Question 2: What is wrong, if anything, with this statement: "Not only should man be God-centered, but God himself is God-centered."

LESSON
4

DAY
1

DAY 2—DEATH

LESSON 4

DAY 2

Death is all around us and we can't do anything to prevent its reality. Ecclesiastes 8:8 tells us "No man has power to retain the spirit, or power over the day of death."

Question 3: How often do you think about death? What is your attitude toward death?

Thinking about death and eternity helps keep God as the center of our lives by testing whether we are more in love with this world than we are in love with God himself. Does the thought of dying give us more pain at losing what we love on earth than it gives us joy at gaining Christ?[10]

Question 4: How could someone glorify God in their death? In other words, what kind of death brings God glory?

DAY 3—PAUL'S THOUGHTS ABOUT DEATH

Question 5: Meditate on Philippians 1:18–23.

18 What then? Only that in every way, whether in pretense or in truth, Christ is proclaimed, and in that I rejoice. Yes, and I will rejoice, 19 for I know that through your prayers and the help of the Spirit of Jesus Christ this will turn out for my deliverance, 20 as it is my eager expectation and hope that I will not be at all ashamed, but that with full courage now as always Christ will be honored in my body, whether by life or by death. 21 For to me to live is Christ, and to die is gain. 22 If I am to live in the flesh, that means fruitful labor for me. Yet which I shall choose I cannot tell. 23 I am hard pressed between the two. My desire is to depart and be with Christ, for that is far better.

What is Paul's eager expectation and hope?

Question 6: How does Paul think that this hope will be realized? In other words, what reason or basis does Paul give for this hope?

LESSON
4

DAY
3

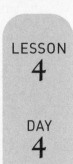

Question 7: What does it mean for Paul to say "to die is gain" (see especially v. 23)?

DAY 4—HEDONISM

Question 8: A dictionary might define hedonism as "a life devoted to pleasure." Given this definition, is hedonism a bad thing? Why or why not?

> I would be happy with the following definition as a starting point for my own usage of the word: *Hedonism* is "a theory according to which a person is motivated to produce one state of affairs in preference to another if, and only if, he thinks it will be more pleasant, or less unpleasant for himself." I would only want to add "forever." For there are deeds God calls us to do that in the short run are painful.[11]

DAY 5—*CHRISTIAN* HEDONISM?

Question 9: What might the term "Christian Hedonism" mean?

> I have found over the years that there is a correlation between people's willingness to get over the offensiveness of the term *Christian Hedonism* and their willingness to yield to the offensive biblical truth behind it. The chief effect of the term is not that it creates a stumbling block to the truth, but that it wakens people to the fact that the truth itself is a stumbling block—and often a very different one than they expected.[12]

Question 10: Interact with this statement: "You shouldn't live a life devoted to pleasure; you should live a life devoted to God."

LESSON
4

DAY
5

FURTHER UP AND FURTHER IN

LESSON 4

Further up and further in

Read *Desiring God*, Appendix 5, "Why Call It Christian Hedonism?"

Question 11: After reading John Piper's rationale for this provocative label, do you agree that it is an appropriate term? Even if you disagree with the term, do you think that what it signifies is biblical and true? Explain your answer.

Read *Desiring God*, Chapter 3, pages 77–92

Question 12: John Piper gives an illustration of worship on page 82. Draw a picture of this illustration and label each part of your drawing:

Question 13: According to John Piper, worship "is a way of
_____ _____ back to God the radiance of _____
_____" (page 84).

Question 14: According to John Piper, what makes worship vain?
What makes worship authentic? Support your answer with the Bible
references that John Piper uses.

Read an Article That Summarizes What Christian Hedonism Is

It can be found at
http://www.desiringgod.org/AboutUs/OurDistinctives/ChristianHed
onism/

Question 15: Summarize what Christian Hedonism is in your own
words.

LESSON
4

*Further up
and
further in*

While You Watch the DVD, Take Notes

**LESSON
4**

*DVD
and
discussion*

What is the central question in this series?

Why is it so important to begin with God's glory?

How does Philippians 1:20–21 support the statement, "God is most glorified in us when we are most satisfied in him"?

John Piper's modification of the definition for hedonism:
 A life devoted to pleasure _____ _____

Why is this modification important?

After You Watch the DVD, Discuss What You've Learned

1. How can we admire the glory manifest in nature or portrayed in movies without becoming idolaters?

2. How are worldly or sinful hedonists different from Christian hedonists? Is every human a hedonist in the broad sense of the term?

3. React to this statement: "Your life's vocation—*as a Christian!*—is to maximize your happiness." If true, does this statement encourage you? Why?

After You Discuss, Make Application

1. Record one thing from this lesson that you want to remember or think more about:

2. Explain what Christian Hedonism is to an unbelieving friend or family member. Record your conversation here:

LESSON
4

*DVD
and
discussion*

PURSUE YOUR JOY: GOD COMMANDS IT!

A Companion Study to *The Blazing Center*, Session 4

LESSON OBJECTIVES

It is our prayer that after you have finished this lesson...

- You will be able to explain why we ought to maximize our joy in God.

- You will learn to honor God by coming to him to meet your needs.

- You will understand the proper role of self-denial.

Before You Watch the DVD, Study and Prepare

DAY 1—JOY COMMANDED

Question 1: Read Psalm 100:1–2.

> 1 Make a joyful noise to the LORD, all the earth! 2 Serve the
> LORD with gladness! Come into his presence with singing!

According to these verses, would it be disobedient to serve the
Lord without joy?

Question 2: Read Philippians 4:4.

> 4 Rejoice in the Lord always; again I will say, Rejoice.

Is this a command? Are you obeying this command?

Question 3: Read Psalm 37:4.

> 4 Delight yourself in the LORD, and he will give you the
> desires of your heart.

According to this verse, would God give you anything
you want, even if it was something sinful? Why or why not?

LESSON
5

DAY
1

LESSON 5

DAY 2

> We are commanded to feel, not just to think or decide. We are commanded to experience dozens of emotions, not just to perform acts of willpower.[13]

DAY 2—THE NATURE OF FAITH

Question 4: Ponder Hebrews 11:6.

> [6] And without faith it is impossible to please him, for whoever would draw near to God must believe that he exists and that he rewards those who seek him.

Is God pleased when we seek a reward from him? Do *you* seek reward from him?

Question 5: How does Hebrews 11:6 define faith?

DAY 3—THE NATURE OF EVIL

Question 6: Consider Jeremiah 2:9–13.

> 9 Therefore I still contend with you, declares the LORD, and with your children's children I will contend. 10 For cross to the coasts of Cyprus and see, or send to Kedar and examine with care; see if there has been such a thing. 11 Has a nation changed its gods, even though they are no gods? But my people have changed their glory for that which does not profit. 12 Be appalled, O heavens, at this; be shocked, be utterly desolate, declares the LORD, 13 for my people have committed two evils: they have forsaken me, the fountain of living waters, and hewed out cisterns for themselves, broken cisterns that can hold no water.

Based on this passage, write a definition of what evil is in your own words:

LESSON

5

DAY

3

LESSON
5

DAY
4

Sin considers God and his glory, and instead of loving God's glory and treasuring God's glory, sin exchanges God's glory for something else. That is what sin is.

Sin has to do with God, mainly. It is not mainly hurting people, though it does hurt people. Mainly, it is dishonoring God. It is belittling his glory—by not trusting him and not treasuring him and not wanting him as the foundation and center of our lives. All have sinned and are exchanging and, therefore, lacking the glory of God and, therefore, dishonoring the glory of God.[14]

DAY 4—THE NATURE OF CONVERSION

Question 7: Look at Matthew 13:44.

44 The kingdom of heaven is like treasure hidden in a field, which a man found and covered up. Then in his joy he goes and sells all that he has and buys that field.

Why would the man in this parable sell all that he has in order to buy the field?

Question 8: This verse mentions that this man sells all that he has *with joy*. How could he be joyful if he is losing all that he has?

Question 9: What does this parable teach us about the kingdom of heaven? Why would Jesus tell this parable to his disciples?

DAY 5—THE PURSUIT OF JOY
AND SELF-DENIAL

The most common objection against the command to pursue joy is that Jesus commanded just the opposite when He called for our self-denial.[15]

LESSON
5

DAY
5

My response to this is to protest that Christian
Hedonism does capture the true Biblical sense of
self-denial and loss of life for the sake of Christ
and the gospel.[16]

Question 10: Read Hebrews 11:24–26.

[24] By faith Moses, when he was grown up, refused to be
called the son of Pharaoh's daughter, [25] choosing rather to be
mistreated with the people of God than to enjoy the fleeting
pleasures of sin. [26] He considered the reproach of Christ
greater wealth than the treasures of Egypt, for he was looking to the reward.

Do these verses describe Moses practicing self-denial? Why or
why not?

FURTHER UP AND FURTHER IN

Read *Desiring God*, Chapter 2, pages 53–63
Question 11: Why would John Piper ask someone if they had
received Jesus as their Treasure rather than asking them if they had
believed in Jesus?

Question 12: How is the gospel presentation on pages 55–63 different from and/or similar to other presentations of the gospel which you have heard?

Read *Desiring God*, Chapter 2, pages 63–74

Question 13: List some assertions about conversion that John Piper makes in this section:

Question 14: How does the entire second chapter of *Desiring God* prove the point that "the pursuit of joy in God is not optional" (page 73)?

LESSON
5

*Further up
and
further in*

LESSON
5

Further up
and
further in

Read the Epilogue to *Desiring God*

Question 15: Of the seven reasons John Piper lists for writing this book, which one was the most confusing to you? If none of his reasons were confusing, which reason prompted the most joy in your heart and why?

While You Watch the DVD, Take Notes

Eight Biblical Arguments for Christian Hedonism
(Write Scripture references next to each argument)

1. God _____ us to be happy and to pursue our joy.
2. God _____ terrible things if we will not be satisfied.
3. The nature of _____ teaches the pursuit of satisfaction in God.
4. The nature of _____ teaches the pursuit of satisfaction in God.
5. The nature of _____ teaches the pursuit of satisfaction in God.
6. The nature of _____ teaches the pursuit of satisfaction in God.
7. The demand to _____ _____ teaches the pursuit of satisfaction in God.

[The eighth argument is a story]

After You Watch the DVD, Discuss What You've Learned

1. How do pursuing joy and pursuing obedience relate?

2. How does self-denial fit into Christian Hedonism and the pursuit of joy?

3. Retell (to someone in your group) the illustration that John Piper uses involving his wife and an anniversary gift of flowers. What does this illustration prove?

After You Discuss, Make Application

1. Record one thing from this lesson that you want to remember or think more about:

2. Choose one of the Scripture references that John Piper mentions in this session to memorize. Choose a reference that impacted you personally. Be prepared to recite it from memory during the next lesson. Record your selection here:

LESSON
5

DVD
and
discussion

TRUE LOVE: DUTY OR DELIGHT? (PART 1)

A Companion Study to *The Blazing Center*, Session 5

LESSON OBJECTIVES

I t is our prayer that after you have finished this lesson...

- You will understand how 1 Corinthians 8 illustrates genuine love.

- You will be able to articulate why joy in God is essential to love.

- You will receive grace from God, enabling you to be a more loving person.

Before You Watch the DVD, Study and Prepare

DAY 1—ISN'T THIS LOVE?

Question 1: Imagine that you are walking on the sidewalk of a city street. You see a young child run into the street to grab something blowing in the wind. But a car is speeding toward the child. A middle-aged man sees the young child and knows that he is going to be hit. So he runs into the street and throws the child out of the way and is hit by the car himself. He dies. Now, is this man's action necessarily an action of love? Defend your answer.

Question 2: Examine 1 Corinthians 13:3.

3 If I give away all I have, and if I deliver up my body to be burned, but have not love, I gain nothing.

Is it possible to give away everything that you have and deliver yourself to be burned, but have not love? How might your answer to this question affect your answer to the previous question?

LESSON
6

DAY
1

This [1 Corinthians 13:3] is a startling text. For Jesus Himself said, "Greater love has no one than this, that someone lays down his life for his friends" (John 15:13). How can Paul say that laying down your life may in fact be a loveless act?

One thing is for sure: Love cannot be equated with sacrificial action! It cannot be equated with *any* action! This is a powerful antidote to the common teaching that love is not what you feel, but what you do.[17]

Question 3: Reconsider the scenario in the first question. What would make the man's action love? What would make the man's action *not* love? Could such an action ever come from a combination of both loving and non-loving motives? Why?

DAY 2—WHAT IS LOVE (AGAIN)?

Question 4: Review Lesson 3, which corresponds to Session 2 of *The Blazing Center*. How did you define love on Day 2 (Questions 3 and 4)? What did John Piper say about love in this lesson? How did he define love?

DAY 3—MACEDONIAN LOVE

Question 5: Read 2 Corinthians 8:1–9.

[1] We want you to know, brothers, about the grace of God that has been given among the churches of Macedonia, [2] for in a severe test of affliction, their abundance of joy and their extreme poverty have overflowed in a wealth of generosity on their part. [3] For they gave according to their means, as I can testify, and beyond their means, of their own free will, [4] begging us earnestly for the favor of taking part in the relief of the saints— [5] and this, not as we expected, but they gave themselves first to the Lord and then by the will of God to us. [6] Accordingly, we urged Titus that as he had started, so he should complete among you this act of grace. [7] But as you excel in everything—in faith, in speech, in knowledge, in all earnestness, and in our love for you—see that you excel in this act of grace also. [8] I say this not as a command, but to prove by the earnestness of others that your love also is genuine. [9] For you know the grace of our Lord Jesus Christ, that though he was rich, yet for your sake he became poor, so that you by his poverty might become rich.

LESSON
6

DAY
3

According to 2 Corinthians 8:6–8, in what two ways does Paul describe the Macedonians' giving?

Question 6: According to these verses, how does God's grace relate to human action?

DAY 4—CHRISTIAN COMFORT?

Question 7: Reread 2 Corinthians 8:1–4.

¹ We want you to know, brothers, about the grace of God that has been given among the churches of Macedonia, ² for in a severe test of affliction, their abundance of joy and their extreme poverty have overflowed in a wealth of generosity on their part. ³ For they gave according to their means, as I can testify, and beyond their means, of their own free will, ⁴ begging us earnestly for the favor of taking part in the relief of the saints.

Does God's grace remove poverty or affliction?

Question 8: Using these verses, how might you respond to someone who was preaching a "health and wealth gospel"—that is, a gospel that declares that it is always God's will for his children to be financially prosperous, healthy, and successful, and that those who aren't lack faith?

DAY 5—THE OVERFLOW OF JOY

Question 9: Read 2 Corinthians 8:1–4 a third time.

> [1] We want you to know, brothers, about the grace of God that has been given among the churches of Macedonia, [2] for in a severe test of affliction, their abundance of joy and their extreme poverty have overflowed in a wealth of generosity on their part. [3] For they gave according to their means, as I can testify, and beyond their means, of their own free will, [4] begging us earnestly for the favor of taking part in the relief of the saints.

How did the Macedonians' joy relate to their giving?

Question 10: If 2 Corinthians 8:1–4 is a description of love (cf. 2 Cor 8:8), then how might you define love based on these verses?

LESSON
6

DAY
5

FURTHER UP AND FURTHER IN

Read *Desiring God*, Chapter 4, pages 111–121

Question 11: State, in your own words, John Piper's explanation of how 1 Corinthians 13:5 does not contradict his thesis that we must pursue our deepest pleasure in order to be loving.

Question 12: Record John Piper's definition of love.

Read *Desiring God*, Chapter 4, pages 121–132

Question 13: Record John Piper's second definition of love. How do his first definition and second definition relate?

Question 14: Can the love of a Christian Hedonist involve weeping and self-denial? Explain.

Read *Desiring God*, Chapter 4, pages 132–141

Question 15: Consider the section entitled, "Love's Deed and Reward Are Organically Related" (pages 137–139). Why is this an important qualification?

While You Watch the DVD, Take Notes

What assertion is John Piper defending in this session?

If you pursue your joy in God you will be a _____ person.

You cannot be a _____ person unless you pursue your joy in God.

2 Corinthians 8:1–4, 8—an illustration of biblical love.
Piper's definition of love:

Love involves more than sheer _____.

LESSON

6

*DVD
and
discussion*

After You Watch the DVD, Discuss What You've Learned

**LESSON
6**

*DVD
and
discussion*

1. If someone insisted on arguing that love is not a feeling, how would you respond?

2. Can an unbeliever love others? Defend your answer.

3.   How has this session freed you to be a more loving person?

After You Discuss, Make Application

1. Record one thing from this lesson that you want to remember or think more about:

2. Think of one specific area of your life in which you lack love. Are you acting dutifully but lacking a joyful heart? Confess this to God, and, if necessary, confess and ask forgiveness from other people. Pray that God would give you the grace to love in this specific area or situation.

TRUE LOVE: DUTY OR DELIGHT? (PART 2)

A Companion Study to *The Blazing Center*, Session 6

LESSON OBJECTIVES

It is our prayer that after you have finished this lesson...

- You will be able to list several texts that demonstrate the need for joy in love.

- You will appreciate the advantage it is to you if those in positions of authority over you serve you in joy.

- You will humbly receive the exhortations to love that are made in this session.

Before You Watch the DVD, Study and Prepare

DAY 1—ISN'T THIS LOVE (AGAIN)?

**LESSON
7**

**DAY
1**

Question 1: Imagine that you are watching an offering plate being passed from person to person in church. The plate is passed to a woman that you know is poor. This person puts a wad of money into the plate, a huge gift from someone that doesn't have that much to spare. Now, is this woman's action necessarily an action of love? Defend your answer.

Question 2: Read 2 Corinthians 9:5–7.

⁵ So I thought it necessary to urge the brothers to go on ahead to you and arrange in advance for the gift you have promised, so that it may be ready as a willing gift, not as an exaction. ⁶ The point is this: whoever sows sparingly will also reap sparingly, and whoever sows bountifully will also reap bountifully. ⁷ Each one must give as he has made up his mind, not reluctantly or under compulsion, for God loves a cheerful giver.

Is it possible to give lots of money, but not to please God? What pleases God in giving?

> I take this to mean God is not pleased when people act benevolently but don't do it gladly. When people don't find pleasure (Paul's word is *cheer*) in their acts of service, God doesn't find pleasure in them. He loves cheerful givers, cheerful servants. What sort of cheer? Surely the safest way to answer that question is to remember what sort of cheer moved the Macedonians to be generous. It was the overflow of joy in the grace of God. Therefore, the giver God loves is the one whose joy in Him overflows "cheerfully" in generosity to others.[18]

DAY 2—THE SECRET OF LOVING GIVING

Question 3: Study Luke 14:12–14.

> 12 He said also to the man who had invited him, "When you give a dinner or a banquet, do not invite your friends or your brothers or your relatives or rich neighbors, lest they also invite you in return and you be repaid. 13 But when you give a feast, invite the poor, the crippled, the lame, the blind, 14 and you will be blessed, because they cannot repay you. You will be repaid at the resurrection of the just."

LESSON
7

DAY
2

What motivation does Jesus provide for giving to the poor? Should our love be motivated by the reward promised to us?

Question 4: Read Acts 20:33–35.

> 33 I coveted no one's silver or gold or apparel. 34 You yourselves know that these hands ministered to my necessities and to those who were with me. 35 In all things I have shown you that by working hard in this way we must help the weak and remember the words of the Lord Jesus, how he himself said, "It is more blessed to give than to receive."

In helping the weak and the poor, why must we *remember* that it is more blessed to give than to receive?

Most Christians today think that while it is true that giving brings blessing, it is not true that one should "remember" this. Popular Christian wisdom says that blessing will come *as a result* of giving, but that if you keep this fact before you as a motive, it will ruin the moral value of your giving and turn you into a mercenary. The word *remember* in Acts 20:35 is a great obstacle to this popular wisdom. Why would Paul tell church elders to *keep in mind* the benefits of ministry, if in fact their doing so would turn ministers into mercenaries?[19]

DAY 3—THE SECRET OF LOVING LEADERSHIP

Question 5: Consider Hebrews 13:17.

[17] Obey your leaders and submit to them, for they are keeping watch over your souls, as those who will have to give an account. Let them do this with joy and not with groaning, for that would be of no advantage to you.

How is it advantageous to you if those in authority over you lead you with joy?

LESSON
7

DAY
3

LESSON 7

DAY 3

Question 6: How might Hebrews 13:17 apply to the way in which you submit to your employer, parents, teacher, government? How can you make their leading joyful?

[T]he Bible says (Ephesians 6:1), "Children obey your parents." Do what they say. Don't lie to them. Next to God the instruction of your parents is the most sacred and important thing in your life. Treat them with great respect. The Bible promises that things will go far better for you if you do.

[T]he Bible says that children are responsible to honor and obey their parents. If they don't there will be trouble, and if they do there will be reward. Children are addressed and children are responsible for their submissiveness and respect.[20]

DAY 4—OUT OF THE COMFORT ZONE

Question 7: In your mind, what is the greatest obstacle (or obstacles) to showing kindness to someone who isn't in your circle of friends? What prevents us from loving those who are different from ourselves?

Question 8: How might contentment in God, or satisfaction in God, remove the obstacle(s) you mentioned in your previous answer?

LESSON
7

DAY
4

DAY 5—BATTLING FOR PURITY OVER PORN

LESSON
7

DAY
5

My conviction is that one of the main reasons the world and the church are awash in lust and pornography (by men and women—30% of internet pornography is now viewed by women) is that our lives are intellectually and emotionally disconnected from infinite, soul-staggering grandeur for which we were made. Inside and outside the church, western culture is drowning in a sea of triviality, pettiness, banality, and silliness. Television is trivial. Radio is trivial. Conversation is trivial. Education is trivial. Christian books are trivial. Worship styles are trivial. It is inevitable that the human heart, which was made to be staggered with the supremacy of Christ, but instead is drowning in a sea of banal entertainment, will reach for the best natural buzz that life can give: sex.

Therefore, the deepest cure to our pitiful addictions is not any mental strategies—and I believe in them and have my own (see ANTHEM[21]). The deepest cure is to be intellectually and emotionally staggered by the infinite, everlasting, unchanging supremacy of Christ in all things. This is what it means to *know* him. Christ has purchased this gift for us at the cost of his life. Therefore, I say again with Hosea, let us know, let us press on to know the Lord.[22]

Question 9: From what you have observed in the battle for purity, what strategies don't work well? In other words, what things are poor motivators for staying pure?

Question 10: As you consider John Piper's definition of love—"the overflow of abundant joy in God that meets the needs of others"— how might this kind of love keep you from sexual sin?

Cultivate the capacities for pleasure in Christ. One reason lust reigns in so many is that Christ has so little appeal. We default to deceit because we have little delight in Christ.[23]

LESSON
7

DAY
5

FURTHER UP AND FURTHER IN

Read *Desiring God*, Chapter 7, pages 192–201

Question 11: Based upon this section, how would you respond to someone who said, "I give a lot of money to the poor. It's not that I care much about the poor. What I really want is the heavenly reward that will come to me for giving to them."

Question 12: How does the wartime lifestyle relate to love and joy?

Read *Desiring God*, Chapter 8, pages 121–132

Question 13: Interact with the opening sentence of this chapter: "The reason there is so much misery in marriage is not that husbands and wives seek their own pleasure, but that they do not seek it in the pleasure of their spouses."[24]

Question 14: How might an unmarried person benefit from reading this chapter?

Read John Piper's Poem for His Wife on Their 25th Wedding Anniversary

It can be found at http://www.desiringgod.org/ResourceLibrary/NarrativePoems/ByDate/1384_For_Noel_On_Our_25th_Wedding_Anniversary/

Question 15: Summarize this poem's teaching on love and Christian Hedonism.

While You Watch the DVD, Take Notes

More biblical descriptions of love:

2 Cor. 9:7–8—Giving is loving if you are _____.

The battle is not first at the level of _____.

LESSON

7

DVD and discussion

The battleground is what makes you _____.

Acts 20:35—The most controversial word in this verse is
"_____."

You _____ with this promise.

Luke 14:12–14—Be motivated by the _____ of your joy as you draw other people into it.

Closing exhortations:

Get outside your _____ _____.

For love's sake say no to _____.

Do something radical for the _____.

After You Watch the DVD, Discuss What You've Learned

1. If John Piper is biblically accurate when he says that joy is essential to love, how would you motivate someone else to do a loving thing? How would you motivate yourself?

2. What superior pleasure must invade your heart in order for you to say no to the lesser pleasure of sexual impurity?

3. After watching this session and the previous one, has your understanding of love changed? If so, how has it changed?

After You Discuss, Make Application

1. Record one thing from this lesson that you want to remember or think more about:

2. Consider the three exhortations that John Piper made at the end of the session: getting outside your comfort zone, saying no to pornography, and doing something for the poor. Choose one of the exhortations to focus on (not that you will ignore the others, however!). Then write down specific and realistic things that you can do to move toward this exhortation. Look over your list and pray to God for the courage and love for carrying your strategy to completion.

LESSON
7

DVD
and
discussion

SUFFERING: FOR THE JOY SET BEFORE YOU (PART 1)

A Companion Study to *The Blazing Center*, Session 7

LESSON OBJECTIVES

It is our prayer that after you have finished this lesson...

- You will comprehend how joy in God enables endurance in suffering.

- You will feel God's call on your life to suffer with Christ.

- You will be ready, by the grace of God, to endure suffering with joy in God.

Before You Watch the DVD, Study and Prepare

DAY 1—YEAH, BUT WHAT ABOUT SUFFERING?

Christian Hedonism is not a message that is only for people without problems, people who have an "easy" life. It is not blind to the loneliness, hurt, sickness, and hardship in the world. Christian Hedonism speaks perhaps most powerfully to those who are suffering. And to them it still speaks its message of joy in God.

> Love is costly. It always involves some kind of self-denial. It often demands suffering. But Christian Hedonism insists that the gain outweighs the pain. It affirms that there are rare and wonderful species of joy that flourish only in the rainy atmosphere of suffering.[25]

Question 1: Read 2 Timothy 3:10–13.

[10] You, however, have followed my teaching, my conduct, my aim in life, my faith, my patience, my love, my steadfastness, [11] my persecutions and sufferings that happened to me at Antioch, at Iconium, and at Lystra—which persecutions I endured; yet from them all the Lord rescued me. [12] Indeed, all who desire to live a godly life in Christ Jesus will be persecuted, [13] while evil people and impostors will go on from bad to worse, deceiving and being deceived.

LESSON
8

DAY
1

LESSON
8

DAY
1

Should every Christian expect to suffer? What specific kind of suffering does Paul expect in these verses? What are some other types of suffering?

Question 2: When someone becomes a Christian, do you think that their suffering usually increases or does it usually decrease? Defend your answer.

DAY 2—LET GOODS AND KINDRED GO

Question 3: Consider Hebrews 10:32–36.

> 32 But recall the former days when, after you were enlightened, you endured a hard struggle with sufferings, 33 sometimes being publicly exposed to reproach and affliction, and sometimes being partners with those so treated. 34 For you had compassion on those in prison, and you joyfully accepted the plundering of your property, since you knew that you yourselves had a better possession and an abiding one. 35 Therefore do not throw away your confidence, which has a great reward. 36 For you have need of endurance, so that when you have done the will of God you may receive what is promised.

How did these believers endure the plundering of their property *with joy?*

Question 4: What was the "better possession" these believers knew they had? If you know that you have a "better possession," what does that free you to do?

DAY 3—CHRISTIAN COMPARISON SHOPPING

Question 5: Imagine that someone walks up to you and offers you one of two options. You can either have $100 today, or if you are willing to refuse the $100 and wait one year, you can have $100,000. Which option would you choose? Why?

Question 6: Read Hebrews 11:24–26.

> 24 By faith Moses, when he was grown up, refused to be called the son of Pharaoh's daughter, 25 choosing rather to be mistreated with the people of God than to enjoy the fleeting pleasures of sin. 26 He considered the reproach of Christ greater wealth than the treasures of Egypt, for he was looking to the reward.

LESSON
8

DAY
3

What two options did Moses have? Which option did he choose? How does the previous question relate to Moses's situation?

> In 1949 when Jim Elliot was a college student he wrote the words that have become the motto of many of our young people at Bethlehem: "He is no fool who gives what he cannot keep to gain what he cannot lose."[26]

DAY 4—LOOKING TO JESUS,
THE MAN OF FAITH

Moses is a mighty example of the life of faith. But there is no better model than Jesus himself. Jesus lived a life of perfect *faith*.

Question 7: Study Hebrews 12:1–3.

> [1] Therefore, since we are surrounded by so great a cloud of witnesses, let us also lay aside every weight, and sin which clings so closely, and let us run with endurance the race that is set before us, [2] looking to Jesus, the founder and perfecter of our faith, who for the joy that was set before him endured the cross, despising the shame, and is seated at the right hand of the throne of God. [3] Consider him who endured from sin-

ners such hostility against himself, so that you may not grow weary or fainthearted.

How did Jesus endure suffering? What enabled him to choose the path of suffering and the cross?

Question 8: Reread Hebrews 12:3. How does considering Jesus bring us endurance for our own trials?

It is not a morally defective thing to be sustained in the marathon of life by the joy of triumph at the end. The reward of seeing God and being free from all sin is the greatest incentive of all.

So if it seems that there are going to be some temporary losses when you run this race with Jesus, you are right. That is why Jesus said to count the cost (Luke 14:25–33) before you sign on. But the marathon of the Christian life is not mainly loss. It is mainly gain. "For the joy that was set before him he endured the cross." It is only a matter of timing. If you see things with the eyes of God, there is a vapor's breath of loss and pain, and then everlasting joy (2 Corinthians 4:17).[27]

LESSON
8

DAY
4

DAY 5—A CALL TO SUFFER WITH CHRIST

Question 9: Finish this survey of the final chapters of Hebrews by looking at Hebrews 13:12–14.

12 So Jesus also suffered outside the gate in order to sanctify the people through his own blood. 13 Therefore let us go to him outside the camp and bear the reproach he endured. 14 For here we have no lasting city, but we seek the city that is to come.

Explain in your own words what is commanded in these verses.

Question 10: What is offered as the motivation for obeying this command?

FURTHER UP AND FURTHER IN

Read *Desiring God*, Chapter 10, pages 253–260

Question 11: How would *you* answer the following question: "What if your life turns out to be based on a falsehood, and there is no God?"

Question 12: Why do you think that John Piper takes a detour (pages 256–260)?

Read *Desiring God*, Chapter 10, pages 260–270

Question 13: Could you, or anyone you know, say, "The lifestyle I have chosen as a Christian would be utterly foolish and pitiable if there is no resurrection"? What would such a phrase mean?

LESSON
8

*Further up
and
further in*

LESSON
8

*Further up
and
further in*

Question 14: State, in your own words, John Piper's explanation of how Paul "fills what is lacking in the afflictions of Christ."

Read an Online Article about Suffering and Shame
It can be found at:
http://www.desiringgod.org/ResourceLibrary/TasteAndSee/ByDate/1999/1133_Embracing_the_Pain_of_Shame/

Question 15: How do you explain the apostles' rejoicing in the midst of suffering (Acts 5:41)? What gave them the power to rejoice and not to wilt under the suffering they had received?

While You Watch the DVD, Take Notes

All of us will experience _____ eventually.

God is most glorified in us when we are most satisfied in him _____ when we maintain joy in him in suffering.

Love really shines as _____ when you press on loving others even when it's really hard and really costly.
The theme of the sustaining power of joy in our suffering in the book

The theme of the sustaining power of joy in our suffering in the book of Hebrews:

Heb. 10:32–34—You have a _____ _____, his name is Jesus.

Heb. 11:24–26—The _____ of Christ is riches.

Heb. 12:1–2—How did Jesus survive the lashes?

Heb. 13:12–14—Here we have no _____ city.

After You Watch the DVD, Discuss What You've Learned

1. Why couldn't a Christian just be content to endure suffering without joy?

2. At one point in his message John Piper makes it clear that the heavenly reward he is speaking of is not a golf course in heaven (or a "bigger heavenly mansion"), but more of Christ. Why is this an important clarification?

LESSON
8

*DVD
and
discussion*

**LESSON
8**

*DVD
and
discussion*

3. Is God calling you to embrace a risk or measure of suffering in your life for his sake? Try to think of a specific example.

After You Discuss, Make Application

1. Record one thing from this lesson that you want to remember or think more about:

2. Write a letter to encourage someone you know who is suffering. Include some of what you've learned in this lesson.

SUFFERING: FOR THE JOY SET BEFORE YOU (PART 2)

A Companion Study to *The Blazing Center*, Session 8

LESSON OBJECTIVES

It is our prayer that after you have finished this lesson...

- You will believe that the cause of Christ is greater than any other cause and worth dying for.

- You will be inspired by the testimonies of those who have suffered with joy in God and confidence in his sovereignty.

- Your heart will surge with a readiness to follow Jesus wherever he might take you.

Before You Watch the DVD, Study and Prepare

DAY 1—ROLE MODELS

Question 1: Who are your role models? Whom do you admire and what do you admire about them? Why do you want to be like them?

Question 2: What difference do role models make in our lives? Do your role models shape who you will be in the future? What's the importance of having godly role models?

There is a simple principle at work in all this which I think everyone in this room can agree to. The principle is this: We become like those we admire most.

I admired honesty in my Dad, so I tried to be honest myself. I liked the pitching style of Mudcat Grant, so it became my style in little league. I thought Lenny Green was cool the way he chewed bubble gum, so I chewed gum just like him. Hannah krinkles her nose because her mommy krinkles her nose.

We become like those whom we admire.[28]

DAY 2—FOLLOW ME AS I FOLLOW CHRIST

Question 3: Read Philippians 3:17–19.

> 17 Brothers, join in imitating me, and keep your eyes on those who walk according to the example you have in us. 18 For many, of whom I have often told you and now tell you even with tears, walk as enemies of the cross of Christ. 19 Their end is destruction, their god is their belly, and they glory in their shame, with minds set on earthly things.

How do verses 18 and 19 support Paul's exhortation in verse 17? What do these verses say about good and bad role models?

Question 4: Read Hebrews 13:7.

> 7 Remember your leaders, those who spoke to you the word of God. Consider the outcome of their way of life, and imitate their faith.

Why does the author of this book urge his readers to "consider the outcome of their way of life"?

LESSON
9

DAY
2

Question 5: Why is the type of imitation the Bible calls for not the same thing as idolatry? How might 1 Corinthians 11:1 be used to answer such an objection?

[1] Be imitators of me, as I am of Christ.

DAY 3—YOUR REAL ROLE MODEL

It's one thing to say that someone is your role model. It's another thing to actually admire and imitate them. In terms of admiration and actual imitation, consider the following questions:

- Whom do you spend the most time admiring or enjoying?

- Who do you most often find yourself wishing you could talk like, write like, think like, act like?

- Whom do you enjoy talking about with your friends?

- If you had spare time to spend with anyone you would want, whom would you choose?

- If your friends had to compare you to someone they knew, to whom would they compare you?

Question 6: After thinking about these questions, would you change your answer to the first question of this lesson? Why?

DAY 4—WHERE GOD IS IN SUFFERING

Question 7: Read Ephesians 1:11–12.

> [11] In him we have obtained an inheritance, having been pre-destined according to the purpose of him who works all things according to the counsel of his will, [12] so that we who were the first to hope in Christ might be to the praise of his glory.

According to these verses, is there anything (including suffering) that is outside of the plan of God?

Question 8: Read Romans 8:28.

> [28] And we know that for those who love God all things work together for good, for those who are called according to his purpose.

LESSON
9

DAY
4

Does this promise apply even to the suffering that we experience in this life?

> This is God's universal purpose for all Christian suffering: more contentment in God and less satisfaction in self and the world. I have never heard anyone say, "The really deep lessons of life have come through times of ease and comfort." But I have heard strong saints say, "Every significant advance I have ever made in grasping the depths of God's love and growing deep with Him has come through suffering."[29]

DAY 5—A CALL TO SUFFER WITH CHRIST (AGAIN)

Question 9: Study Philippians 3:7–11.

7 But whatever gain I had, I counted as loss for the sake of Christ. 8 Indeed, I count everything as loss because of the surpassing worth of knowing Christ Jesus my Lord. For his sake I have suffered the loss of all things and count them as rubbish, in order that I may gain Christ 9 and be found in

him, not having a righteousness of my own that comes from the law, but that which comes through faith in Christ, the righteousness from God that depends on faith— [10] that I may know him and the power of his resurrection, and may share his sufferings, becoming like him in his death, [11] that by any means possible I may attain the resurrection from the dead.

According to these verses, how is it possible to have joy in the midst of suffering?

Question 10: Study 1 Peter 1:3–9.

[3] Blessed be the God and Father of our Lord Jesus Christ! According to his great mercy, he has caused us to be born again to a living hope through the resurrection of Jesus Christ from the dead, [4] to an inheritance that is imperishable, undefiled, and unfading, kept in heaven for you, [5] who by God's power are being guarded through faith for a salvation ready to be revealed in the last time. [6] In this you rejoice, though now for a little while, as was necessary, you have been grieved by various trials, [7] so that the tested genuineness of your faith—more precious than gold that perishes though it is tested by fire—may be found to result in praise and glory and honor at the revelation of Jesus Christ. [8] Though you have not seen him, you love him. Though you do not now see him, you believe in

LESSON
9

DAY
5

him and rejoice with joy that is inexpressible and filled with glory, 9 obtaining the outcome of your faith, the salvation of your souls.

What do these verses add to what you answered in the previous question?

FURTHER UP AND FURTHER IN

Read *Desiring God*, Chapter 10, pages 270–279

Question 11: According to this section, how is the suffering of God's people related to the spread of his gospel?

Question 12: When you read the stories of Dansa, Natasha, and Josef, how does it affect your heart? What is God stirring in you as you read these accounts?

THE BLAZING CENTER STUDY GUIDE   95

Read *Desiring God*, Chapter 10, pages 279–288

Question 13: List four sources of joy in the midst of suffering that are set forth in this section:

Question 14: Fill-in-the-blank: "In the pursuit of _____ through _____, we _____ the all-satisfying worth of the Source of our joy" (page 288).

Read an Online Article About Suffering and Dying
It can be found at
http://www.desiringgod.org/library/fresh_words/2000/101000.html.

Question 15: What verse from the Bible will be on your lips as you die?

While You Watch the DVD, Take Notes

Examples of a "cool" life from WWII:

The story of _____ _____

LESSON
9

*Further up
and
further in*

"You are living for something _____ times more _____ than winning the Second World War."

"Let me be like that, Lord, for the cause of _____."

The story of _____ _____

"Suffering is not only the _____ you will have to pay in the pathway of obedience sustained by joy in God, suffering is also _____ by God to _____ your joy in him."

His purpose in suffering is to refine you like _____.

Illustrations of the sovereign use of suffering to deepen joy in God:

Joni Eareckson Tada

Steve Saint

The Backstroms

After You Watch the DVD, Discuss What You've Learned

1. Is the American church ready to hear a call to lay down its life, to be involved in the front lines of the battle? Is your church? Are you? Why or why not?

2. Do you know of any testimonies of Christians who have endured suffering with joy in God? Share them with the group.

3. If someone knew that they had poor role models who were influencing them, either directly or indirectly, to live a wasted life, how would you counsel them to find and develop new role models? Whom would you encourage them to imitate?

After You Discuss, Make Application

1. Record one thing from this lesson that you want to remember or think more about:

2. Choose a missionary biography to read. If you don't know of one you might want to try *Bruchko* (by Bruce Olson) or *Shadow of the Almighty* (by Elisabeth Elliot). Record your selection here:

LESSON
9

*DVD
and
discussion*

REVIEW AND CONCLUSION

LESSON OBJECTIVES

It is our prayer that after you have finished this lesson…

- You will be able to summarize and synthesize what you've learned.

- You will hear what others in your group have learned.

- You will share with others about your joy and God's glory.

WHAT HAVE YOU LEARNED?

There are no study questions to answer in preparation for this lesson. Instead, spend your time writing a few paragraphs that explain what you've learned in this group study. To help you do this, you may choose to review the notes you've taken in the previous lessons and especially the things you've recorded in every application section. Then, after you've written down what you've learned, write down some questions that still remain in your mind about anything addressed in these lessons. Be prepared to share these reflections and questions with the group in the next lesson.

NOTES

Use this space to record anything in the group discussion and interview clips that you want to remember:

LESSON
10

LEADER'S GUIDE

As the leader of this group study, we feel that it is very important for you to be familiar with this study guide and with *The Blazing Center* DVD set. Therefore, we highly recommend that you (1) read and understand the introduction, (2) that you skim each lesson, surveying its layout and content, and (3) that you read the entire Leader's Guide *before* you begin the group study and distribute the study guides. Reading John Piper's *Desiring God* would also be an excellent investment for you as the group leader. Many of the concepts in *The Blazing Center* are covered in detail in this book.

Additionally, you may find yourself at times wanting to supplement or modify the contents of this study guide. Please do not feel constrained by any of the study questions, meeting schedules, or worksheets contained in this resource. Remember that this guide is a resource; any additions or changes you make that better match the study to your particular group are deeply encouraged. As the group leader, your own prayerful and faith-filled discernment, creativity, and guidance are invaluable, and you should adapt the material as you see fit. We would be thrilled if, by God's grace, his Spirit would use the things in this study guide as a springboard to direct you to new and fresh ways to engage your group.

LEADING PRODUCTIVE DISCUSSIONS[30]

It is our conviction that the best group leaders foster an environment in their group which engages the participants. We learn by solving problems or by working through things that provoke curiosity or concern. This study guide is meant to facilitate an investigation into biblical truth—an investigation that is shared by the group leader and the participants. Therefore, we encourage you to adopt the posture of a "fellow-learner" who invites participation from everyone in the group.

It might surprise you how eager people can be to share what they have learned in preparing for each lesson. Therefore, you should invite participation by asking your group participants to share their discoveries. Here are some of our "tips" on facilitating discussion that is engaging and helpful:

- Don't be uncomfortable with silence initially. Once the first participant shares their response, others will be likely to join in. But if you cut the silence short by prompting them, then they are more likely to wait for you to prompt them every time.
- Affirm every answer, if possible, and draw out the participants by asking for clarification. Your aim is to make them feel comfortable sharing their ideas and learning, so be extremely hesitant to "shut down" someone's contribution or "trump" it with your own. This does not mean, however, that you shouldn't correct false ideas—just do it in a spirit of gentleness and love.
- Don't allow a single person, or a few persons, to dominate the discussion. Involve everyone, if possible, and intentionally invite participation from those who are more reserved or hesitant.
- Labor to show the significance of their study. Emphasize the things that the participants could not have learned without doing the homework.
- Avoid talking too much. The group leader should not monopolize the discussion, but rather guide and shape it. If the group

leader does the majority of the talking, the participants will be less likely to interact and engage, and therefore they will not learn as much. Avoid constantly adding the "definitive last word."

- The group leader should feel the freedom to linger on a topic or question if the group demonstrates interest. The group leader should also pursue digressions that are helpful and relevant. There is a balance to this, however: The group leader *should* attempt to cover the material. So avoid the extreme of constantly wandering off topic, but also avoid the extreme of limiting the conversation in a way that squelches curiosity or learning.

- The group leader's passion, or lack thereof, is infectious. Therefore, if you demonstrate little enthusiasm for the material, it is almost inevitable that your participants will likewise be bored. But if you have a genuine excitement for what you are studying, and if you truly think Bible study is worthwhile, then your group will be impacted positively. Therefore, it is our recommendation that before you come to the group, you spend enough time working through the homework and praying, so that you can overflow with genuine enthusiasm for the Bible and for God in your group. This point cannot be stressed enough. Delight yourself in God and in his Word!

BEFORE LESSON 1

Before the first lesson, you will need to know approximately how many participants you will have in your group study. **Each participant will need their own study guide.** Therefore, be sure to order enough study guides. You will distribute these study guides at the beginning of the first lesson.

Again, we highly recommend that you, as the leader, familiarize yourself with this study guide and *The Blazing Center* DVD set in order to answer any questions that might arise, and also to ensure that each group session runs smoothly and maximizes the learning of the participants. It is not necessary for you to preview *The Blazing Center* in its entirety—although it certainly wouldn't hurt!—but you should be prepared to navigate your way through each DVD menu. For instance, during the first lesson you will be playing two brief clips from the interview portion that is included on Disc 3 as part of the bonus features. The interview clips can be accessed by choosing the third option on the root menu of Disc 3 and then the first option of the subsequent menu, entitled "John Piper Interview." You should be prepared to show these two clips during the first lesson.

DURING LESSON 1

Each lesson is designed for a one-hour group session. Lessons 2–10 require preparatory work from the participant before this group session. Lesson 1, however, requires no preparation on the part of the participant.

The following schedule is how we suggest that you use the first hour of your group study:

Introduction to the Study Guide (10 min)
Introduce this study guide and *The Blazing Center* DVD. Share with the group why you chose to lead the group study using these resources. Inform your group of the commitment that this study will

require and motivate them to work hard. Pray for the ten-week study, asking God for the grace you will need. Then distribute one study guide to each participant. You may read the introduction aloud, if you want, or you may immediately turn the group to Lesson 1 (starting on page 9 of this study guide).

Personal Introductions (15 min)

Since group discussion will be an integral part of this guided study, it is crucial that each participant feels welcome and safe. The goal of each lesson is for every participant to contribute to the discussion in some way. Therefore, during this fifteen minutes, have each partici- pant introduce themselves. You may choose to use the questions listed in the section entitled, "*About Yourself*," or you may ask ques- tions of your own choosing.

Discussion and Interview Clip #1 (15 min)

Transition from introductions to the first set of discussion questions listed under the heading, "A Preview of *The Blazing Center*." Invite everyone in the class to respond to these questions, but don't let the discussion become too involved. These questions are designed to "start the gears turning." The aim is not to come to definitive answers yet. After several minutes, conclude the discussion and play the first question and answer from the bonus features section of Disc 3. The question for this clip is entitled, "What is your prayer for this series?" After watching this two-minute clip, ask the group participants for their reaction. Did they understand what was said? What do they have questions about? What did they find interesting? Replay the clip if necessary, or pause the clip for discussion. Remember, this brief clip and the brief discussion before and after the clip are meant to introduce the series, to stimulate thought, and to whet the appetite for more study. You may inform the students that this ten-week study will argue for the prominence of the emotions (and joy) in biblical Christianity.

Discussion and Interview Clip #2 (15 min)

After approximately fifteen minutes, invite discussion on the second set of questions. Then play the eighth question and answer from the bonus features section of Disc 3. The question for this clip is entitled, "Are teenagers too young to understand these things?" The clip is about a minute long. After it is finished, ask the group participants for their reaction again. Conclude the discussion by stressing that this DVD series will argue that you never have to choose between being happy and doing the right thing. In fact, God demands that you pursue your own happiness.

Review and Closing (5 min)

End the group session by reviewing Lesson 2 with the group partici-pants and informing them of the preparation that they must do before the group meets again. Encourage them to be faithful in preparing for the next lesson. Answer any questions that the group may have and then close in prayer.

BEFORE LESSONS 2-9

As the group leader, you should do all the preparation for each les-son that is required of the group participants, that is, the ten study questions. Furthermore, it is highly recommended that you com-plete the entire "Further Up and Further In" section. This is not required of the group participants, but it will enrich your preparation and help you to guide and shape the conversation more effectively.

The group leader should also preview the session of *The Blazing Center* that will be covered in the next lesson. So, for example, if the group participants are doing the preparatory work for Lesson 3, you should preview *The Blazing Center*, Session 2 before the group meets and views it. Previewing each session will better equip you to understand the material and answer questions. If you want to pause the DVD in the midst of the session in order to clarify or discuss, previewing the session will allow you to plan where you want to take your pauses.

When all is taken into account, you should be ready to plan for about two hours of your own preparation before each lesson.

DURING LESSONS 2–9

Again, let us stress that during Lessons 2–9, you may use the group time in whatever way you desire. Nevertheless, the following schedule may help you by providing a basic starting structure:

Discussion (10 min)

Begin your time with prayer. The tone you set in your prayer will likely be impressed upon the group participants: if your prayer is serious and heart-felt, the group participants will be serious about prayer; if your prayer is hasty, sloppy, or a token gesture, the group participants will share this same attitude toward prayer. So model the kind of praying that you desire your group to imitate. Remember, the blood of Jesus has bought your access to the throne of grace.

After praying, review the preparatory work that the participants completed. How did they answer the questions? Which questions did they find to be the most interesting or the most confusing? What observations or insights can they share with the group?

The group participants will be provided an opportunity to apply what they've learned in Lessons 2–9. As the group leader, you can choose whether it would be appropriate for the group to discuss these assignments during this ten-minute time slot.

DVD Viewing (30 min)

Play the session for *The Blazing Center* that corresponds to the lesson you're studying. You may choose to pause the DVD at crucial points to check for understanding and provide clarification. Or, you may choose to watch the DVD without interruption.

Discussion and Closing (20 min)

Foster discussion on what was taught during John Piper's session. You may do this by first reviewing the DVD notes (under the heading "While You Watch the DVD, Take Notes") and then proceeding to the discussion questions, listed under the heading "After You Watch the DVD, Discuss What You've Learned." These discussion questions are meant to be springboards that launch the group into further and deeper discussion. Don't feel constrained to these questions if the group discussion begins to move in other helpful directions.

Close the time by briefly reviewing the application section and the homework that is expected for the next lesson. Pray and dismiss.

BEFORE LESSON 10

It is important that you encourage the group participants to complete the preparatory work for Lesson 10. This assignment invites the participant to reflect on what they've learned and what remaining questions they still have. As the group leader, this would be a helpful assignment for you to complete as well. In addition, you may want to write down the key concepts of this DVD series that you want the group participants to walk away with.

You have the option of showing some of the interview clips during Lesson 10, so ensure that you are familiar with Disc 3 and how the interview clips can be accessed.

DURING LESSON 10

The group participants are expected to complete a reflection exercise as part of their preparation for Lesson 10. The bulk of the group time during this last lesson should be focused on reviewing and synthesizing what was learned. Encourage each participant to share some of their recorded thoughts. Attempt to answer any remaining questions that they might have.

When you finish the discussion of their assignment, you may choose to select the "John Piper Interview" option on Disc 3 of *The Blazing Center*. We suggest that you allow the participants to choose which questions they want to hear John Piper answer. Play the interview clip and then discuss what was said. Play as many interview questions and answers as you have time for.

To close this last lesson, you might want to spend extended time in prayer. If appropriate, take prayer requests relating to what the participants have learned in these ten weeks, and bring these requests to God.

It would be completely appropriate for you, the group leader, to give a final charge or word of exhortation to end this group study. Speak from your heart and out of the overflow of joy that you have in God.

To every group leader who chooses to use this study guide, please receive our blessing:

The LORD bless you and keep you; the LORD make his face to shine upon you and be gracious to you; the LORD lift up his countenance upon you and give you peace. (Numbers 6:24–26)

NOTES

1. This phrase is borrowed from John Piper.
2. While the DVDs contain only eight sessions, this study guide adds an introduction and conclusion session for the benefit of groups. Although this resource is designed to be used in a group setting, it can also be used by the independent learner. Such a learner would have to decide for themselves how to use this resource in the most beneficial way. We would suggest doing everything but the group discussion, if possible.
3. Excerpt taken from http://www.desiringgod.org/ResourceLibrary/Sermons/ByDate/1991/780_He_S aw_the_Grace_of_God_and_Was_Glad/
4. Excerpt taken from http://www.desiringgod.org/ResourceLibrary/ConferenceMessages/ByDate/145 7_Is_God_for_Us_or_for_Himself/
5. Excerpt taken from *Desiring God*, page 57.
6. Excerpt taken from *Desiring God*, pages 41–42.
7. Excerpt taken from *The Pleasures of God*, page 11.
8. Excerpt taken from http://www.desiringgod.org/ResourceLibrary/Sermons/ByDate/1992/792_God_ Predestined_Us_unto_Sonship_Through_Jesus_Christ/
9. Excerpt taken from http://www.desiringgod.org/ResourceLibrary/Sermons/ByDate/1998/1054_The _Other_Dark_Exchange_Homosexuality_Part_2/
10. Excerpt taken from http://www.desiringgod.org/ResourceLibrary/Sermons/ByDate/1993/845_What _Happens_When_You_Die_At_Home_with_the_Lord/
11. Excerpt taken from *Desiring God*, pages 365–366.
12. *Desiring God*, 368.
13. Excerpt taken from *Desiring God*, page 300.
14. Excerpt taken from http://www.desiringgod.org/ResourceLibrary/Sermons/ByDate/1999/1079_The _Demonstration_of_Gods_Righteousness_Part_2/
15. Excerpt taken from *Desiring God*, page 295.
16. Excerpt taken from http://www.desiringgod.org/ResourceLibrary/Articles/ByDate/1993/1537_A_Re sponse_to_Richard_Mouws_Treatment_of_Christian_Hedonism_in_iThe_God _Who_Commandsi/

17. Excerpt taken from *Desiring God*, page 116.
18. Excerpt taken from *Desiring God*, pages 120–121.
19. *Desiring God*, 125.
20. Excerpt taken from
    http://www.desiringgod.org/ResourceLibrary/Sermons/ByDate/1988/637_He_
    Must_Manage_His_Household_Well/
21. John Piper's ANTHEM strategies against lust can be found at the Desiring God
    website at the address,
    http://www.desiringgod.org/ResourceLibrary/TasteAndSee/ByDate/2001/1187_
    A_N_T_H_E_M/
22. Excerpt taken from
    http://www.desiringgod.org/ResourceLibrary/ConferenceMessages/ByDate/184_
    Sex_and_the_Supremacy_of_Christ_Part_2/
23. This excerpt is part of the "E" (ENJOY a superior satisfaction) strategy for
    fighting lust that is one of six strategies forming the acronym ANTHEM. See
    footnote 20 for the web address.
24. *Desiring God*, 205.
25. Excerpt taken from *Desiring God*, page 129–130.
26. Excerpt taken from
    http://www.desiringgod.org/ResourceLibrary/Sermons/ByDate/1984/454_My_
    Name_Is_God_Almighty/
27. Excerpt taken from
    http://www.desiringgod.org/ResourceLibrary/Sermons/ByDate/1997/1005_Run
    ning_with_the_Witnesses/
28. Excerpt taken from
    http://www.desiringgod.org/ResourceLibrary/Sermons/ByDate/1985/483_We_S
    hall_Be_Like_Him/
29. Excerpt taken from *Desiring God*, page 265.
30. This material has been adapted from curricula produced by The Bethlehem
    Institute (TBI), a ministry of Bethlehem Baptist Church. It is used by
    permission.